The Light of the World

The Life of Jesus for Children

KATHERINE PATERSON • FRANÇOIS ROCA

SCHOLASTIC INC.

New York Toronto London Auckland Sydney
Mexico City New Delhi Hong Kong Buenos Aires

This book is for Madison Ruth Yohanan and
Gina Catherine Paparella—new lights in our dark world.

— K. P.

To Charlotte, my ray of light.

— F. R.

ISBN-13: 978-0-545-10444-9

ISBN-10: 0-545-10444-0

Text copyright © 2008 by Katherine Paterson. Front cover illustration copyright © 2008 by François Roca. Illustrations copyright © 1998 by Bayard Editions Jeunesse, from *Jésus pour les petits*, by Marie-Hélène Delval, illustrated by François Roca. All rights reserved. Published by Scholastic Inc. SCHOLASTIC, the LANTERN LOGO, and associated logos are trademarks and/or registered trademarks of Scholastic Inc.

Arthur A. Levine Books hardcover edition published by Arthur A. Levine Books, an imprint of Scholastic Inc., January 2008

12 11 10 9 8 7 6 5 4 3 2 1   8 9 10 11 12 13/0

Printed in the U.S.A.   40

First Scholastic paperback printing, November 2008

Book design by Leyah Jensen

*T*he *Bible* *tells* *us* that in the beginning, when God created the heavens and earth, there was nothing but darkness until God said: "Let there be light." And there was light.

Many years ago, the prophet Isaiah lived in a dark time for his country. The wise king of Judah had died, and powerful enemies threatened to destroy his tiny land. But Isaiah believed God's promise that the people who were living in darkness would someday see a great light.

This is the story of light coming into the world.

In the town of Nazareth, there lived a young woman whose name was Mary.

One day, to her amazement, an angel visited her. "Mary," he said. "Don't be afraid. God is delighted with you. He has chosen you to be the mother of a special child. You are to name him 'Jesus.' He will be great. Indeed, he will be called the 'Son of God.'"

Mary was engaged to a man named Joseph, who was a carpenter. They traveled to Bethlehem, where her baby was born, not in a house or hotel, but in a stable.

That night, out in the dark countryside, shepherds watched over their sheep. Suddenly, a blinding light shattered the darkness. The shepherds were terrified. Out of the light, an angel spoke to them: "Don't be afraid. I bring you good news of great joy for all the world. The Savior you have been waiting for has been born in Bethlehem." The shepherds ran to town, where they found Mary and Joseph and the baby, who was lying in a manger. They praised God and told everyone what they had seen and heard.

Wise men in faraway lands saw a star and followed its light to the place where Jesus was. When they saw the baby, they fell down and worshipped him, and gave him rich gifts, fit for a newborn king.

Mary and Joseph returned to their home in Nazareth, where Jesus grew up.

When Jesus was about thirty years old, he left his work as a carpenter in Nazareth, and began the work for which he had been born. He showed God's love by healing those who were sick and making friends with those who had no friends. People came from far and wide to meet him and hear the good news of God's love for them.

Jesus invited others to join him in his work. Twelve of them became his close companions. They were called "disciples" because they followed him and looked to him as their teacher. Together, Jesus and his disciples traveled through the towns and countryside, telling everyone about God's kingdom.

The people only knew of kings and rulers whose power was selfish and cruel. But Jesus explained that God's kingdom was not like the kingdoms on earth. God, Jesus said, is like a shepherd who has a hundred sheep, but when he realizes that one of them is missing, he searches everywhere until he finds it. How happy he is to put his lost sheep on his shoulders and carry it home to safety.

Of course the people were eager for a kingdom where the ruler is a kind shepherd, but Jesus said they could not see it yet. The coming of God's kingdom, he said, is like the seed that a farmer scatters on his land. After many days, like a miracle, the seed begins to grow—first a bit of stalk, then the hint of green leaf, until finally the plant is tall and the grain is ripe. At last his crop is ready for harvest.

Jesus taught about God's kingdom of love in actions as well as words. There was a man who was paralyzed. One day four of his friends carried him to see Jesus. When Jesus saw him lying on the ground, he said to the man, "Stand up and walk." The man stood up and walked home with his friends. Those who saw this were amazed and praised God.

This was the work that Jesus had been born for—to make the lame walk, to make the blind see, and to preach to the poor and friendless the good news of God's loving kingdom.

One day when Jesus was teaching, people brought children to him, hoping that he would pray for them. Jesus' disciples tried to stop this interruption, but Jesus said, "Let the children come here to me. You must not keep them away, because it is to them and those like them that the kingdom of God belongs. The truth is that unless you receive the kingdom of God like a little child, you'll never enter it at all." And he put his arms around the children and blessed them.

Jesus wanted his disciples to understand that they too were to show God's love. "You are the light of the world," he told them. "Let your light shine so that people can see your good works and give glory to your Father in heaven."

Most people were amazed by Jesus' words and his acts of healing. "Surely," they said, "this man could not do the things he does unless God was with him."

But others were angry about the things Jesus said and did. "It is against the law for someone to call himself the 'Son of God,'" they said. "Anyone who does that should die."

At this time Jesus told his friends that he had to go to Jerusalem, which was the capital. The people were thrilled to see him there, for they believed their king was coming to claim his new kingdom. They waved palm branches, singing, "Blessed is he who comes in the name of the Lord!"

But Jesus was not coming to claim his kingdom. Later that week, he gathered his closest friends to celebrate the feast of Passover. When they were at the table, Jesus broke a loaf of bread and gave the pieces to each of them. "This bread is like my body," he said, "which I am giving for you." Then he took a cup of wine and passed it around the table. "Drink from this cup, all of you, for this wine is like my blood, which will be poured out for many people." The disciples did not understand what Jesus meant. They could not believe Jesus was telling them that he was going to die.

After supper Jesus went to a garden to pray. He was brokenhearted because he knew what was going to happen.

Soon soldiers arrived. They arrested Jesus and took him to Pilate, who was the ruler of the country. The people turned against Jesus. When Pilate asked the crowd what he should do with him, they cried out, "Crucify him! Crucify him!"

Jesus was hung on a cross on a hill outside the city, between two men who were thieves. His frightened friends had run away. He felt very alone.

When Jesus died, darkness covered the earth. The light of the world had gone out.

A rich man who admired Jesus laid his body in a tomb. A great stone was rolled across the entrance.

Two days later, women who had loved Jesus went to visit his burial place. They were astounded to see the stone rolled away and an angel in dazzling clothes standing beside the empty tomb. The women were terrified, but the angel said to them, "Do not be afraid. You are looking for Jesus of Nazareth, who was crucified. He is not here. He has risen from the dead."

After that, Jesus' friends saw him many times. But even after he went away to heaven, they knew his Spirit was always with them. The light had come into the world, and not even the darkness of death could overcome it.

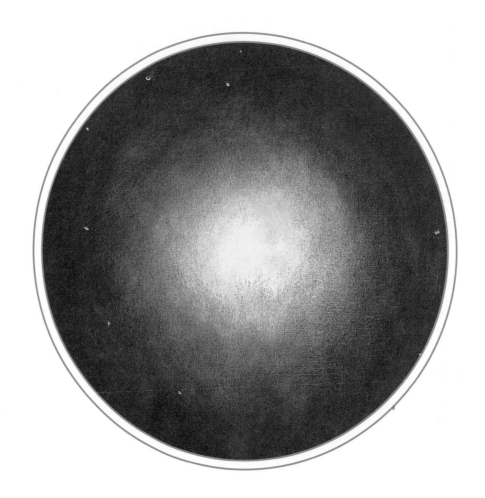

The light still shines through everyone who, like Jesus, lives the good news of God's loving kingdom.